Tara's Journey

A Story of Faith and Encouragement

Betty J. Peters

Pat, Chuck & Family,
We thank you for all the prayers, caring, love and concern on behalf of our family. May God be with each of you and grant stable health and much happiness.
Our Love, The Peters Family

The Brauer Family,

Psalms 18:1-6 sums up the story God gave me pretty well. Verses 4-6 aren't for me just about physical death but also spiritual death to the world and self so I could have Spiritual life through Jesus!!! God bless you always!!!

Love in Him,
Tara Peters

DORRANCE PUBLISHING, CO., INC.
PITTSBURGH, PENNSYLVANIA 15222

All Rights Reserved
Copyright © 2000 by Betty J. Peters
No part of this book may be reproduced or transmitted
in any form or by any means, electronic or mechanical,
including photocopying, recording, or by any information storage
and retrieval system without permission in
writing from the publisher.

ISBN # 0-8059-4913-5
Printed in the United States of America

First Printing

For information or to order additional books, please write:
Dorrance Publishing Co., Inc.
643 Smithfield Street
Pittsburgh, Pennsylvania 15222
U.S.A.
1-800-788-7654

In honor of our daughter, Tara.
We have been blessed by her beauty,
courage, and strength.
Also dedicated to my husband, Ron,
and son, Derek, in thankfulness for their
overwhelming love and support.

Contents

Preface

Writing this book should have taken place shortly after Tara's illness in 1989 was made known to us. Many times I have said it was a dream of mine to write and publish a book. I wrote down some things, but many, many thoughts were left unsaid; only the heart and mind had these memories stored for future reference. Hopefully, now the dream will become reality.

I used to think small, minute events which took place were really big events, but have learned since what I thought were worries, were not worries at all. One learns as you go along the journey of life, very much like the words in a song of a few years back: Life is like a dance, you learn as you go. How true this is and how much we really do learn and still never know everything about to happen, not to mention the events about which we worry that never materialize.

Since Tara's diagnosis, we have grown as a family. We are closer to each other, have developed a more meaningful relationship with God, are thankful for old friends, and are grateful for the many new friendships we have made, along with being more humble.

You realize that the strength is given to you, no matter what comes your way. God gives this strength when we often times are unaware of how He watches over us. The phrase we have heard many times, God never gives us anything our shoulders are not broad enough to handle, is true. We think they are burdens to deal with, but they turn out to be the best challenges for us to get through, only with God's guidance. The mountains we climb give rewards in their own special way.

The coping mechanisms are different for each person, and he or she handles stress in his or her own fashion. Some members of our family bottle up their feelings, others will share from time to time, and some of us will just simply spit out what is troubling us. Myself, I can only hold it in so long and then must express how I feel, or at least try to give it to our creator, as only He is big enough to take it away from us. We learn there are certain things we do not have any control over. He holds the key to everything in our lives. We must give it all back to Him, sit back, and try to wait patiently for the answers of what will take place.

We say we give it all to God and yet still keep attempting to solve matters on our own. It doesn't work! All things must be in His time and in His way. Only He knows best, knows what the future holds, and has the missing pieces of the overall puzzle of our lives.

The blue sky, sunrises and sunsets, green grass, budding trees, freshly fallen snow, and spring showers all take on new meaning. Now even birds chirping catch our attention, when we did not always notice what beautiful singing we could enjoy in our own backyard. We have a candle holder which says, Each of life's seasons has its own special beauty.

The caring of family and friends helps to lighten our days and fill our moments of doubt with hope. No one can say we did it all alone. We have not gotten to this stage without love and concern being expressed, prayers said, heard, and answered with God's miracle in the journey of Tara's life and our lives.

Footprints

One night a man had a dream. He dreamed he was walking along the beach with the Lord. Across the sky flashed scenes from his life. For each scene, he noticed two sets of footprints in the sand; one belonged to him, and the other to the Lord.

When the last scene of his life flashed before him, he looked back at the footprints in the sand. He noticed that many times along the path of his life there was only one set of footprints. He also noticed that it happened at the very lowest and saddest times in his life.

This really bothered him and he questioned the Lord about it. "Lord, you said that once I decided to follow you, you'd walk with me all the way. But I have noticed that during the most troublesome times in my life, there is only one set of footprints. I don't understand why when I needed you most you would leave me."

The Lord replied, "My precious, precious child, I love you and I would never leave you. During your times of trial and suffering, when you see only one set of footprints, it was then that I carried you."

Chapter One

Blind Date

Ron and I first were introduced by mutual friends for a blind date, went out on two dates, and each went our own way. I guess it was not meant to be at that particular time. Neither of us married in the meantime, and as fate would have it, six or seven years later we met again in the bank parking lot. Actually, God brought us together for a second time, and we have been with only each other since that eventful day. I had worked late that afternoon, and Ron was at the bank tending to some affairs as I was cashing my paycheck. Ron ordinarily did not do business at this certain bank, so was this a coincidence or what that placed us there at exactly the same time?

God had plans for us and placed us in a situation with a second encounter. With his great wisdom, He knew best and showed us we were best as a pair.

We dated for a year and married on August 2, 1975. The biological clock was ticking, as we were in our thirties and both truly wished for children in our lives to share our home. Just ten and a half months after our wedding, God blessed us with a beautiful baby girl on June 12, 1976 at 4:01 A.M. This much-wanted precious baby we named Tara Lynn, and how we treasured her. An hour after birth, the nurse brought Tara to my bedside and asked, "Do you want your daughter?" Did I want our baby to hold? Certainly! Even with no sleep for the night, I eagerly took Tara in my arms. Her eyes were as blue as the ocean, and wide open, looking into my face. There is no greater feeling in the world that tops the birth of your children. This high for the parents is hard to explain and nothing means as much to them; it is truly God's most precious gift!

Finally, the wonderful husband, home, and family I had prayed for were given to me. I felt really blessed! I quit my job as a medical transcriptionist to stay at home and be a full-time mom. This decision was oh-so-wise and gave the greatest pleasures above and beyond anything Ron and I had experienced in our entire lives.

Two years later, on June 29, 1978 at 12:36 P.M., we were again blessed with a handsome baby boy whom we named Derek Ronald. If we thought we were blessed with the birth of our first child, the arrival of Derek brought double blessings. Our happiness could not be put into words. God had been so good to us; he'd given us a girl and a boy, the opportunity to raise one of each, the joys along with the difficult times.

Derek was a pure bundle of energy. He had big brown eyes, was always alert, and full of adventure. We welcomed him openly into our home and hearts, as did big sister Tara, who was delighted to have a baby brother.

Should there be any question as to whether or not blind dates are the thing, the matchmaker sister and brother team of our friends, Jeanene and Dave, who helped to bring us together as a couple, did okay on our behalf. We have since told them our family has grown from two to four. Our thanks and gratitude to them for introducing us in the very beginning of our relationship.

Little did we know what was lying ahead. Our daughter's life was to be threatened. We would have the task of trying to cope with the unknown while remaining positive, knowing God would give us the strength for endurance. This was to be the hardest thing we have ever had to encounter, and only with His guidance could we even come close to dealing with the totally unexpected—the beginning of the end of anything which resembled so-called normality in our lives.

Chapter Two

Our Family

We are the Peters family, Ron, Betty, Tara, and Derek, who live in a small rural community in mid-Michigan. Our lives were so-called "normal" until right before our daughter's thirteenth birthday. Bicycling and walking was something we did together as a family, and this is how our problem came to the surface and changed our world dramatically. Tara had extreme shortness of breath in April of 1989 while we were walking on the weekend.

This episode hit me right smack in the face. I wondered why a twelve-year-old girl could not do exercise and routine activities without such distress in every day living.

In January of 1989, Tara entered a gym class and could not jog around the gym longer than forty-five seconds, and the teacher had told her to go as long as she could. I heard what she had told me, but trying not to be overly concerned, I didn't really comprehend the seriousness of it all.

Well, that weekend was truly a rude awakening, and I knew immediately something was seriously wrong with Tara. I went back to our house crying about what we had just witnessed.

Tara knew something was wrong with her in the fifth grade, although she didn't know exactly what! Her class had seen a movie in which a man couldn't get from the parking lot to his workplace without shortness of breath. When we finally told her she needed to go to the doctor, Tara said, "No." We said it was very necessary to do so and were going as soon as we could get an appointment.

Our visit to the pediatrician, Dr. Philippon, was set up the first part of the week and also led us to the x-ray department at our local hospital. The technician, Kris, proceeded with the echocardiogram study, (the use of ultrasound to visualize internal cardiac structure. All cardiac valves can be visualized and the dimensions of each ventricle and the left atrium can be measured). Kris then stopped the machine, announced that a cardiologist, Dr. Nelson, was in the building, and had him paged to come to the department. He arrived, accompanied by a medical student, and observed the echocardiogram findings as it was being done. Kris later apologized to me for doing it this way, that is, calling the doctor, and I told her not to be sorry for anything as she had done exactly what she should have done. I asked her if she observed these findings often and her reply was, "Not in a twelve-year-old around this area." She has since said, "I couldn't do this one alone, as it was too upsetting." The caring and concern of this special person will be remembered by an anxious mom, although I was trying not to be in a state of panic, especially for the sake of Tara. I knew I had to remain cool, calm, and collected as much as possible, so she would not be too alarmed with the testing being done.

At the point of Dr. Nelson being called, my gut feeling knew this was a biggie. Usually the test is performed, the final report sent to Dr. Philippon, and then the family notified of the findings. In this case, the findings were known right away.

That very same day after the echocardiogram, I called my husband to accompany Tara and me to the pediatrician's office. I did not want to hear the anticipated bad news without him being at our side. The doctor had already received a call from the hospital and was aware of the situation. As Dr. Philippon examined Tara, listening and listening to her heart, you could hear a pin drop; it was almost deathly quiet. He then told Tara they had found something wrong with her heart. One thing which was special was that he looked right at Tara as he talked to her and definitely included her with this news. He didn't talk over or around her, as she was not a small child. She was only a child about to enter her teenage years with hopes and dreams of growing up and doing her own thing. She had plans for college, a career, and someday a home and family of her own to share her life.

The news had to be scary to Tara and certainly was to her parents. We did have questions and some doubts as to her growing up, much less achieving her goals and dreams.

Dr. Tim Nelson

Chapter Three

Early Childhood

Tara's being as a baby and toddler was very typical and without event healthwise. She was a rather late walker but so lively and active in every way. When she did take those first steps and got underway with walking, we did notice very slight shortness of breath, but it was certainly not a focus, and we did not think of it as something of concern.

Preschool years were spent learning the usual things children experience. When entering school at age five she was very shy, and it was not easy to leave home. It seemed there was silent crying for several days, according to her kindergarten teacher. One day I said, "Tara, you would make Mom real happy if you did not cry in school today." Shortly thereafter Tara bounced off the school bus, ran up the driveway, into the house, and announced, "Mom, I did not cry today!" From then on, school was looked upon as a challenge, with dedication to the fullest with her studies, and parent-teacher conferences were filled with praise about Tara being such a hard worker.

It was then time for sixth grade school camp, the first time away from home. Upon driving home, we will never forget the look on Tara's face. The expression was thought to be a homesick look, but now, looking back, this was the beginning of what was about to surface in the declining health of our young daughter. A chaperone, Mrs. Gates, has since shared with us that Tara explained, "It is a long way up those stairs." Others at the dining area kept asking Tara why she wasn't eating; also there were late arrivals to the events, but Tara simply could not keep up with the other classmates physically.

At the same time, Tara was playing softball in the summer leagues and even was put in to pitch on a few occasions. She finally was unable to run the bases after her bat connected with the ball. We did have concerns as to why the energy level and breathing difficulties were more prominent and noticeable.

Looking back there were telltale signs which were not recognized then but now are very clear as we live these over and over in our minds. At the time, there would have been no help as far as lung transplantation in pediatric patients. This last resort ditch effort was so new and still in the experimental stage even when Tara did actually undergo her lung transplant.

Maybe it was a blessing in disguise not knowing the diagnosis. It gave us a couple of years more in which we were free of worry, thinking all was okay in our world.

Chapter Four

Somehow It Will All Be Made Better

In trying to get help for Tara, our first hospital referral was in Lansing, Michigan. Here they performed the cardiac catheterization (passage of a plastic tube into the heart through a blood vessel for the purpose of obtaining cardiac blood samples, detecting abnormalities, and determining intracardiac pressure). Prior to the procedure, Tara's dad and myself were called into a conference room and the doctor stated, "Do you know this could be it right here today?" What a question to be hit with, and at this time we didn't know if she would make it through the procedure or if we would be bringing her home in a hearse! Hiding our tears from Tara was impossible, and she said afterwards that she wondered why we were crying.

Our minister at the time, Chuck, accompanied us to the hospital as he had done for the initial doctor's office visit in Lansing. He offered us great comfort by just being there when we certainly needed some tender loving care and understanding of the situation, that is as if anyone could try to understand why this was happening. One nurse who had been with us throughout the day and who was very compassionate as she went about her work made a point of not leaving at the end of her shift before she had acknowledged how she felt. With tears streaming down her face, she stated, "I wish there was something more I could do." Didn't we all wish that very same thing!

After the cardiac catheterization, Tara was diagnosed with primary pulmonary hypertension; putting it in simple terms, high blood pressure of the lungs. A rare and fatal disease, it had caused her heart to become tremendously enlarged from being overworked, and the decreased lung function was destroying the heart. The prognosis was not good and the only hope for survival was a heart-lung transplant. Without this Tara would die!

Was that bit of news ever a terrific blow to us as a family; it was almost as though someone had hit us over the head with a hammer! Once we realized this was the way it had to be and we had to accept this situation, we proceeded on with appointments in our search for an answer in treatment for our daughter. Somewhere out there and with all this modern technology, someone had to be able to fix everything.

Tara did say, "I don't want a new heart, I want the one you gave me." Such insight for a youngster of almost thirteen. She has since said, "I don't know what made me say that." Possibly the comment was said in context as to what would actually take place at the time of surgery. The big man upstairs had it all worked out!

Chapter Five

A Very Special Place

The journey led us to Cleveland Clinic and The University of Michigan for evaluations. Lung transplantation was fairly new and still experimental, so we kept looking for a facility where they had performed more of these miraculous surgeries.

With prior medical records having been sent, Children's Hospital of Pittsburgh in Pennsylvania was Tara's next evaluation. There we were met by a warm, compassionate staff and the caring they extended was beautiful; for example, "Hi, you must be the Peters family, and you don't look sick, Tara." The condition of patients with lung problems is deceiving and often they don't appear seriously ill. After going through the evaluation process, with Dr. Beerman and Dr. Armitage reviewing past medical records, and being accepted by the hospital transplant team as a candidate for transplantation, Tara was put on the nationwide transplant list in October of 1989. We were filled with hope and very grateful for the hospital and doctors God had led us to in our attempt to achieve the much needed transplant.

Our son, Derek, was eleven at the time, and the support he gave us was great. His humor along the way as we traveled from one transplant center to another in our search helped brighten our days. He had a few coins in his pocket which periodically would find their way to the desk tops and tap quietly in an attempt to relieve the mind from worry, if only for a short time. Derek, knowing how Tara gasped for air, also knew how to be concerned about his sister in his own special way. All of this had not escaped him, and he too had concerns which he did not express to any of us; it almost seemed as if he had to protect us and not be another person for us to be worried about. We were worried about how all of this would affect him in the overall process of coping big time with what we all had in store for us in the future.

Without our Alma United Methodist Church family giving of themselves with love and overwhelming support, we question how we would have made it through. They embraced us thoroughly, and did we feel that special bond they shared with us ! Tara would attend church when she was able to do so, accompanied by the "green monster" or the "silver streak," as she referred to the oxygen tanks which she hauled behind her. It is bad enough to see an older person having to use oxygen, but it seems especially hard to see such a young person in need of assistance in breathing and just trying to live. Ron just reminded me of Tara being concerned about the gurgling of the water hooked to the oxygen tank and the possibility it might disrupt the sermon or quiet prayer time. We told her there wasn't a person in the church who would be bothered by the sound, only thankful for her being able to be present to worship among them. Church was so important in our lives, and we felt privileged to be with such caring friends.

Having faith is so important in not only good times but also when the crisis occurs, and then it is needed more than we ever thought possible. The prayers were numerous; the situation was too big for us to handle alone, and we knew we had to give it to God. Our lives were all in His hands.

Tutoring for school was done at home for Tara as we waited for thirteen and a half months for the organs to arrive, which were given in Love by a very special family.

Chapter Six

Virginia, Reaching Out

We have a beautiful friend from our church who reached out to us in a way no one can adequately describe. This very special lady is Virginia Shimunek, and we do love her more than she can possibly know.

When we were up against hard times with unknown medical costs, upcoming living expenses away from home, wondering what would be for job security, and generally needing help, here came Virginia to our rescue. There was fund-raising started by her to an endless degree! To our local communities and residents, we give you our thanks and gratefulness always for the way in which you embraced Tara and our whole family.

All of this was made possible by none other than Virginia. As it is known, her reaching out was not asked for or expected in any way, it was done only out of love to a family in need. How many people would step up and tackle such a project all by herself? That's our Virginia! There were endless hours and miles driven, telephone calls, visits to businesses, and whatever else is involved in such an endeavor. There were events taking place on the sidelines which we could not comprehend and which certainly humbled us deeply.

In the midst of all this, there was even a Tara Peters Day planned. A local businessman, Mr. Smith, gave a portion of the proceeds from his businesses for the entire day of activities to Tara's fund. This day included movies, bowling, golfing, and roller-skating for everyone to enjoy. What a giving on his behalf, filled with lots of love and concern for our family.

There was a Powder Puff football game between the St. Louis prison and Ionia prison in Tara's honor. She was given flowers, a football with all the players' names on it, and a sum of money so Tara could receive a much-loved recliner chair. Tara rocked vigorously in this chair and looked out the big picture window at the traffic from the highway. Across from the highway in front of our house is a woods, and there is a farmhouse just north of the woods that is just as pretty and comforting to her as the woods. Tara says, "The fall has always been a pretty season as the tree leaves change from vivid green to vibrant golds, reds, and orange colors. Truly people can see God's hands at work during the fall. It's like God taps the trees with His finger, which is like a master paintbrush." Tara loves the fall season, and it is her favorite time of the year.

Our family was unaware of just how much people cared for us. Many knew us and many did not! The fund was set up at our local bank and also newspaper articles on follow-up occasions were written by Alex, Claudia, Linda, and Adam. They are still read by concerned friends and acquaintances wanting to know of Tara's progress and health status. Several people have told us how much they appreciate the updates and look forward to reading the newspaper stories.

Virginia had illness in her very own family, including her son, Gary, who had been ill since he was a very small child. At the time Virginia was reaching out to help our family, it was unknown yet to her what was to come, that her very own son would later be in need of a heart transplant. This blessed event took place on Virginia's birthday. What better gift could any mother and family members receive than the gift of life! Gary received a new heart. He and his wife, Kathy, together have watched their three daughters grow with new hope for the future. They have been blessed beyond measure by the donor family. Also, Virginia and her husband have had big time heart problems. She had spent time away from home while loved ones were hospitalized and knew of the expenses a family has under these circumstances. At one time, her son and husband were hospitalized together in a large hospital, and she was visiting both of them, which had to be stressful and nerve-wracking.

By walking this road herself, Virginia was well aware of how upsetting these circumstances can be. The bills keep rolling in at home, plus the added expense of living away from home while lending support to recuperating loved ones in hospitals.

Virginia and our whole family.

We will be forever grateful to our friend for just being the person she is: warm, caring, sharing, loving, beautiful inside as well as outside, not only helping us financially but spiritually too! What a gem of a friend; once in a lifetime does one come along who can touch our lives and countless others.

Our love to you, Virginia, and may God richly bless you as you extend yourself in oh-so-many ways to many people. You are Loved.

Chapter Seven

Hope for the Future

After attending church on Sunday, Tara would very often say, "Dad, go by the high school." Yes, indeed her dad would honor that wish and by the school we would go, knowing it was a goal of Tara's to be there once again as a student.

I would say, as any mother also shares those wishes for their children, "Tara, you will walk back through those doors again." Somehow, I felt almost certain that would be the case and this is what kept us all hopeful.

During the summer of 1989, while still being evaluated at the University of Michigan, following evaluation at the Cleveland Clinic, our family of four did take a short vacation to our beloved Charlevoix in Michigan. We had managed to go to "Charlevoix the Beautiful" every other year, and we all loved this very special resort area. Here we had a corner room of always the same motel, The Lodge, that overlooked the lake. We could see the boats coming and going on the lake, then they would go under the bridge which opened and closed throughout the day and night. What a sight to behold. We also took long walks along the pier, put everything aside, and enjoyed the peacefulness of not having to time anything or be anywhere at any given moment.

Tara and Derek, accompanied by their dad, spent many good times in the motel indoor pool getting refreshed by the cool water. I preferred to either read, sunbathe on the deck, watch the boats, or take a much-loved walk downtown. There were art fairs, people hustling and bustling, ice cream cones to be eaten, homemade fudge to buy from a shop where you could see the fudge actually being made, and people just being laid back and away from the hectic pace of the so-called normal living.

For our eating out, away from the cooking, dishes, and all that goes with preparing and planning meals constantly, there was a variety of unique restaurants to enjoy. Upon arriving the first day, after getting settled in the motel and the car unpacked, we would all proceed to walk along with many tourists down the hill in front of the hotel, over the bridge, to the one-of-a-kind pizza establishment, The Village Inn. We always walked wherever we went, except we would drive to the beach one day while we were there. Down the street was a family restaurant, J.R.'s, where we had an oh-so-good breakfast, usually about noon, as we were not early risers on vacation. Dinner was at a restaurant, the Parkside, overlooking the harbor, and they had the best whitefish we have ever eaten!

As our vacation was winding down, all of us wanting to stay longer and not wanting to leave the next day, we would splurge at an exquisite restaurant on the channel. This was one of the highlights for us, and we felt privileged for such a luxury.

During our stay in Charlevoix, our son asked his dad, "If Tara goes kaput, will we ever come back here?" This must have been a concern, knowing full well he could lose his sister. His dad answered this hard question, saying, "We will have to wait and see, but we probably would."

As we loaded the car, packing our belongings and taking our feelings with us regarding the unknown future about how many family members would still be existing in our household upon our next visit, we left our beloved Charlevoix room and headed to the gas station at the edge of town.

Derek and his dad were filling up the car while Tara and I remained inside and shared how we didn't want to leave. We were all dealing with such mixed emotions, each one carrying their thoughts, and it was impossible to know the feelings each was experiencing, even those of the men who were not as open to express what might be troubling them. I looked to the back seat at Tara and tearfully said, "Don't you ever give up the thought that you will be back here."

By this time we had made it from the month of April, being given a diagnosis, visiting two big medical centers, and now anticipating our evaluation in Pittsburgh, Pennsylvania.

We drove to Pittsburgh in October, met with a very well-qualified staff, and decided this would be our final stop in pursuing a transplant center to meet our overwhelming needs. We awaited the decision from Children's Hospital while back home to see if they would accept Tara for transplantation. The letter arrived stating Tara was a good candidate and they would place Tara in the seventy-three percent survival rate. She was now placed on the nationwide transplant list, and we started our wait for the organs. This wait took thirteen and a half months and we were chomping at the bit, wondering if Tara could last long enough for the organs to come.

Chapter Eight

Oxygen and the Long-awaited Call

While being confined to home, the oxygen tank being pulled behind Tara when she went for blood tests or attended church, or tubing hooked up to the oxygen concentrator installed in our home day and night, became a way of life at the age of thirteen years! The hum of the oxygen apparatus became almost unheard, except sometimes as a constant reminder of how necessary this was for survival with the deteriorating health and extreme shortness of breath.

As Tara's condition worsened, in the fall, with Dad having temporary work at present, and Mom working full-time as the carrier of our insurance, a careperson was hired to stay with Tara until one of us came home. It was so difficult for me to go out that driveway each morning, wanting to be with our daughter, knowing the need to hang on to that health insurance, and questioning how long Tara had left to be here with us. I had the constant fear that she would die when we were not at home with her but instead out working and paying a person to do what we should have been doing!

On the way to and from work. I would see healthy teenagers walking along, drinking their pop, and eating snacks, and I would wonder why our daughter was at home, unable to do these pleasures of normal living.

Tara has since said how hard it was for her to stay at home, not attending school, seeing her brother Derek get on the bus every day, ride his bike, play ball, etcetera. It takes a special person to endure such a heavy load and especially when being very ill, but Tara did it with grace and dignity.

The first call for possible organs came on Thursday, November 15, 1990 at 10:15 P.M., but Dr. Griffith called us back, stating the organs could not be used. He then told us, "You tell Tara we are going to see her through this." Our thoughts were, *Have we missed our chance and will another call come in time?* Tara's condition was deteriorating and we knew the need was great. God, however, was not giving up! Just two days later, Saturday, November 17, 1990, the second call came from Dr. Armitage at Pittsburgh at about 11 P.M., and this time it was a go, so off we went! The air ambulance from Ann Arbor, Michigan, met us at the Lansing, Michigan, airport and flew us to Allegheny County Airport in Pittsburgh. We were met by a ground ambulance, and Tara was rapidly transported to the hospital. We had a four-hour time frame from the time of the call to our home to get to the hospital, as the organs can only be kept viable for a certain length of time. Needless to say, everyone was in a dither and more than slightly frazzled with all the arrangements.

Our minister, Chuck Grauer, had recently relocated to Lansing and wanted us to call him when the organs came. He would meet us at the airport. We did call him and just as he said, our caring Chuck arrived, prayers were offered, and spiritual support given. What a friend! We will always thank him and remember the image of him standing and looking up as our air ambulance ascended high into the sky, our destiny certainly unknown as for life.

At the time of our flight, what was unusual about our unknown pilot, later discovered to be Don Farrough, was that he was the son of Rosie, a nurse who worked at the same hospital where I was employed. We did not know this at the time when I hugged and thanked him at the Pittsburgh airport. As Tara was undergoing surgery, I called my boss, Peg Boyd, to inform her of our whereabouts and stated, "Tara is in surgery right now."

Upon hearing this news, Peg said, "I know."

Bewildered as to how this was possible, I then asked, "How do you know?"

She replied, "Do you know who your pilot was? He is Rosie's son."

This made it even more special, as there were close ties to home and acquaintances we knew. It seems mother and son had spoken on the phone; Don said he was tired and needed to sleep as he had been up all night transporting a girl who needed a heart-lung transplant from Ithaca to Pittsburgh. Rosie said, "Tara

Peters!" The reply must have been "Yes." That is how this information had come to surface. This was another turn of events which would not always happen, only in a few instances.

We have heard that the day following Tara's surgery, the excitement and enthusiasm was meaningful throughout the entire hospital for a Monday work day.

Our niece, Martha, her youth minister husband, Bob, and baby Sarah from near Philadelphia came to lend support and love to the four of us for several days. They arrived the same day as Tara was undergoing surgery, and were we thrilled to see them! We will never forget how they embraced us at such a trying time in our lives.

Back in Michigan, our niece, Beth, Martha's sister, was assisting Aunt Marilyn and Uncle Clarence with taking our car from the airport to our home. This was of great help, and we appreciated their kindness in this regard.

Uncle Dave, Aunt Audrey, and their family from Florida were calling and sending cards, as were both sets of grandparents. Most of all, they were all sending prayers to God for each and every one of us.

Yes, we definitely were not alone; so many people were with us in spirit!

Chapter Nine

God's Miracle

Upon arriving at Children's Hospital in Pittsburgh and being met by Dr. Jay Fricker, a terrific cardiologist, and after further testing was done, we were told they could not use the donor's heart that was coming! This bit of news was staggering to us, not knowing if they would use the lungs and then have to find a heart later or what. We were certainly not in the know of what happens in these situations. Here again we just had to trust their judgment and know they were doing the right thing. All of this being so very new to us, we certainly had to leave a whole lot of decision-making to those who were more knowledgeable than we were, and we did have all kinds of belief that we were definitely in the right facility for such a life-threatening illness. We did feel they knew what to do about restoring health to the best of their ability, and we felt that their ability was top notch for transplant centers.

On Sunday, November 18, 1990, Tara received God's miracle, a double lung transplant. With the new lungs, Tara's own heart was healed and reduced to a normal size in a very short time. This remarkable event gave the doctors the knowledge that with the diagnosis of primary pulmonary hypertension, the whole heart-lung block is not always needed. The heart will heal itself with new lungs; it is certainly amazing how this is possible.

As Tara had remarked earlier at such a young age—her wish to have her own heart—God allowed her to keep the heart she was given at birth. It is almost ironic how the pieces of the puzzle were put together in such fashion. Only our creator could have possibly planned all this, His master plan!

While Tara was undergoing surgery, Ron, Derek, and I were given a room in the Intensive Care waiting room area, praying for

God to be with the doctors and give them the knowledge they needed for survival. We also prayed about whatever His wishes were for our family and the outcome for the future. We had such mixed emotions, as periodically someone would come and inform us of Tara's progress: She is now prepared for the actual incision making; we now have the right lung removed, next we will remove the left lung; the new lungs are in place and functioning; and finally, Tara is doing well and will now be going to the recovery room. A family in waiting is not just left in the dark to "sweat it out," the staff could not be more caring, informative, and in general giving us so much love along the way.

It seemed far longer than the eight or nine hours since we had bid Tara goodbye as she was leaving for the surgical suite and the impending procedure. After being observed in the recovery room for a while, we were then taken to the intensive care unit where we observed Tara for the first time. What a sight and very scary! There were tubes coming out of everywhere, machines clicking, people scurrying in every direction, and bells ringing. We were allowed only a short time for each visit so the routine care that needed to be done for Tara was able to be carried out.

As the days followed, Tara was heavily sedated. They did not wake her up because, as they informed us earlier, it is better to let a patient wake up on her own. Teams of interns and residents were outside Tara's room, discussing her progress, and in general taking in the results of her not getting the total heart-lung block which was expected in most cases, but instead receiving only the lungs. It was definitely a learning experience for this teaching university hospital, and one doctor said to us a couple of days or so later, "Congratulations, she has come this far!" It would not have been surprising if Tara had not made it to this point! It was so encouraging to her family and also to the entire staff, as they do have many who die, either on the operating table or during the recovery period. The ones who make it begin the healing process, which is long, trying, and demanding both for the patient and family as well. It is hard to see your loved one at such a low point and then miraculous to watch them slowly progress to where they can be up and about, even with wobbly legs.

While Tara was still in ICU and with diminished appetite, the nurse, Bev, went on her lunch break and brought Tara back a piece of pepperoni pizza; maybe three bites were taken and then she went back to resting again. This was just an example of the tender loving care so freely given to both patient and family.

Soon to follow would be the big step of being transferred to the transplant floor.

Chapter Ten

Donor Family

Following the surgery and while she was still in ICU, Tara's courage and strength was beautiful and uplifting to those around her and certainly encouraging to our family. While still hooked up to the respirator, unable to yet speak, the first words she mouthed to us were, "I want to run!" as her fingers moved, as if running. With a spirit like that, how can you lose? She had courage that simply would not end, and her spunk helped her family more than she will ever know. There were ups and downs, good days and not so good days, but Tara seemed to take it in stride and make the most of each day. Some days she was really sedated with morphine, etcetera, and her eyes would roll back in her head. This sort of got to all of us especially to her brother Derek. At one point he said, "I've got to get out of here!" At times it was difficult for all of us but we all wanted to share in Tara's recovery and be as supportive as we knew how to be, learning as we went along daily.

Telephone calls were coming from back home to check on all of us. There were some rooms at the hospital for families of ICU patients where we stayed for the attempted sleep at night. These were very handy in that we were close to Tara, could call ICU at any time, or check at the nursing station if we had concerns. I remember we were all cozy in the small quarters, but they were adequate accommodations, and we were thankful for a place to bunk for the night. Sleep was restless. I would awaken after fitful sleep for a few short hours, and think of how brave Tara had been through all of it. A few tears would hit the pillow, I'd look around and see my husband and son sleeping at the time, quietly leave the room, and head for ICU where I would inquire if it was possible to go in and see Tara. If report was not taking place at shift change or they were working on Tara, I was granted a visit to help set my mind at ease, just knowing she was okay. Laura Hangard, our social worker, was working on getting us a room at the Ronald McDonald House, as we could only use the hospital room while Tara was in ICU, then had to find another home. Thinking of moving farther away from the hospital at night was a little frightening. We wanted to stay as close as possible, yet knew we must separate ourselves just a tad for some much needed rest. As the time went on, our fears of something going wrong lessened somewhat, and we were able to relax a little.

Tara was taken out of the ICU four days following surgery, on Thanksgiving Day, and assigned a room on 9 North, the transplant floor. Bev, the nurse of whom we had grown fond in ICU, wheeled Tara to the new floor and wished us all well as we thanked her for being so special to us. Other nurses had cared for Tara too, and we conveyed our thanks to them as the opportunity came about. We were grateful to everyone who had helped in any way to make us feel comfortable and free of worry, as much as it was possible not to be apprehensive at certain times, depending how the complications could arise so quickly. We knew we were in good hands and felt safe still confined to the hospital where it was necessary to be for care and recuperation.

What a Thanksgiving blessing we had received, and we were very grateful to the donor family. They gave the greatest gift of all, the gift of life! Their son had been in an automobile accident and had no brain function. The decision must have been made to donate his organs in order to help others live. Maybe it was their wish to have something good come out of their loss, but I can't imagine how one would respond at such a difficult time in losing your child under any conditions, especially so sudden. As we were rejoicing in our happiness, we in no way forgot there was a family who was grieving the loss of a son and maybe a brother, grandchild, nephew, or friends who could not understand why such a loss took place. As parents to lose a child must be as devastating as anything can be; it should be that our children outlive us, but that does not always happen. We grieved for their loss and asked why any of this had to happen. Someone must die to let your child or loved one live!

Without God none of this would have been possible, but it had to be in His time and His way. Words are not enough to express how we really feel in regards to our donor family. We have communicated with them on several occasions through our special transplant coordinator, Lynne Cipriani. Some recipients and donor families do meet, and such a touching and special time that would be. This would have to be in agreement with both families, and I would definitely be in favor of this. Not everyone feels the same way, so each family handles it in their own way. This meeting would have to take place on your own; usually hospitals do not help with this because of confidentiality.

Without their beautiful expression of love in giving their son's organs, Tara may very well have not been here with us.

It is so difficult to choose words to write to the donor family, as they no longer have their son. Our daughter is here only because a part of their son lives on in her life. Even though our letters were sent anonymously, we couldn't just receive those precious lungs without letting them know our gratitude and sincere thanks in making such a decision to share their loss so others may live. It was such a generous act of caring when they had to be hurting more than they had ever hurt in their lives.

There is a tremendous shortage of organs being donated, in comparison to those on the nationwide transplant lists and daily many people are dying before they receive a second chance for life. There is no greater gift one can give and the reward of satisfaction in knowing you have given renewed health and hope for the future to several recipients has to be a comfort in your hours of grief.

The following poem, *One Special Gift,* was written by our family and dedicated to the donor family in honor of their son, who still lives on with Tara and to whomever else he may have given extended life.

May God richly bless you as you have blessed others. We are forever grateful to you!

One Special Gift

When my lungs and heart went bad
It was known new organs needed to be had
We waited over a year
Our thoughts were nothing but fear

We listened so long for the call
God carried us so we would not fall
Thursday, 10:15 P.M. the call came in
This time the plane's engines did not spin

Saturday, two days later, 11:30 P.M., again the call came in
This time the plane's engines went into a spin
As we flew into the night
Our feelings were tight

So beautiful and clear the sky
We were still asking "why"
Thousands of stars so way up high
The unknown was questionable with a sigh

A special boy and his family did give
So a special young girl could live
Even though the donor family has much strife
It is comforting they gave *The Gift of Life*

Derek, Dr. Griffith (Tara's Surgeon), Tara, Betty, and Ron

Chapter Eleven

Dr. Bartley Griffith, Great Surgeon

As for Tara's surgeon, Dr. Bartley Griffith, we highly regard his God-given skills, his own determination and fierce drive for excellence in his field of transplantation, his very special way of responding whenever we see him, and the unending hours he gives to helping others get well. One time, while we were praising his ability, he said, "I am just a little wheel in a big machine." He did not say, "Look at how wonderful I am." He meant that it is a team effort, not just one person is responsible for the achievements. This statement seemed to us that he was a humble man, knowing it was not just him alone in the big circle of events.

Tara had given Dr. Griffith a card which said, "I owe you one million dollars." For the simple fact that she did not have one million dollars, the card then said, "I give you a million THANKS!" We could never, ever repay Dr. Griffith for all he has done for our entire family. How grateful we are to have such a competent surgeon; he is certainly at the very top of the list as far as we are concerned. Without Dr. Griffith, Tara's destiny could have been a much different story, and we will always feel indebted to him for his expertise in lung transplantation.

On our last office visit prior to the anticipated departure from Pittsburgh to back home to Michigan, we were told by Lynne Cipriani, transplant coordinator, that she had a message from Dr. Griffith. He said, "Don't let them leave before I get there." Dr. Griffith had just done a transplant during the previous night, and he didn't want to miss us. Even though he may have been fatigued, this was not portrayed to our family. He wanted pictures taken with Tara and our entire family and arranged the huge stuffed bear he placed between Tara and himself. These pictures are priceless and have their place of honor in Tara's photo album.

On follow-up visits back to Pittsburgh, once in a while we would make an attempt to see him. If he happened to be in his office, he welcomed Tara to step in and visit briefly with him. This very busy man never seemed too swamped to take a few minutes to chat with our family. Never did we feel we were holding him up or in the way! He is one very special person who means so much to four members of our family and countless other families.

Tara's high school graduation arrived; what a huge milestone! With the senior pictures taken, several were shared with our very special friend. He acknowledged how well he liked them with a friendly hug, his genuine smile, and "Thank you!" With our mission accomplished—the special opportunity to share with him our joy and excitement—we then left him to continue his hectic pace. Dr. Griffith definitely played a role in this most meaningful time in Tara's extended life.

Somewhere in his schedule with surgeries, patient follow-up, making rounds with residents, and numerous conferences throughout the world, he must have some time for sports or whatever he enjoys doing for pleasure and relaxation. Finding time for his family is also very important to him, as we understand he is a terrific family man.

For the conferences Dr. Griffith attends, we have heard he shares the results of Tara's X-ray findings before and after the lung transplant, showing the reduction in size of that huge heart which went back to normal size in stages. After only five days, on the X-rays it had already become smaller. Tara asked Dr. Griffith, "Could you see my heart go down in size before you stitched me up?"

He replied, "Yes, somewhat." What a truly remarkable sight for him to see and an example of God's miracle which took place right before their eyes! It was believed this could happen but we don't know if they had actually seen it happen before or not. With this finding they discovered that taking the old lungs out and replacing them with new ones relieved the pressure on the heart and allowed it to go back to normal function. The different transplant centers all share in information gathered at their facilities with one another. Each patient is a piece of the big puzzle that the doctors are trying to put together to understand how to treat upcoming patients to a better degree.

We have the utmost respect and admiration for Dr. Griffith for who he is, a great surgeon and friend whom we will always treasure! We do love you, Dr. Griffith!

Brother Derek, age 12

Chapter Twelve

Brother Derek's Strength

Derek went to school in Pittsburgh very near to the Ronald McDonald House, our home away from home. He was homesick and sometimes would express that he wanted to go home. He would have been home without us; and we all wanted to be there for Tara, as it involved the whole family.

Derek wrote on one of his school papers, "I want to be there for my sister Tara," such mixed emotions for twelve-and fourteen-year-old children in realizing why all this was happening.

Tara had said, "I could go through the surgery, but I couldn't do what Derek did." Not knowing anyone, he presented himself to a strange school in a big city. Derek has always made friends easily but this was a totally different set of circumstances. Needless to say, we were all extremely proud of him for giving of himself in love for his sister.

So Derek would not feel left out or think the whole focus was on Tara, we assured him often that if he was the one being sick, we would do exactly the same thing for him. Even with the difficult times, it has brought us all closer together as a family.

Back home in his own school and environment, still very supportive of Tara with cares and concerns, we have all seen Derek's growth in handling the tough spots of life. Most youngsters are not met by such challenges and worries are much less in dimension by far. For his efforts in this regard we will always thank him for his constant love and presence in our lives.

Without a doubt his experiences of meeting life at most trying times have made him more compassionate towards other people with limitations and struggles as they face the real world. His health is appreciated, and the renewed health of sister Tara is precious to him.

At one time while we were in Pittsburgh for a duration of five weeks and Tara receiving extensive treatment for rejection, Derek was in school at home and stayed with a classmate. Chris and his parents, Pat and Sue. They opened their home and hearts to Derek. We thank them for their love and caring for our family!

Once again they both can board the school bus, attend school at home together, are away from hospital life for longer periods of time, and can regroup with old friends, and we remember always the love shown to us wherever we might call our home. The new friendships along the way will remain as treasures to hold dear and near to each of us.

Chapter Thirteen

Big Milestones

Since Tara was only the second pediatric double-lung transplant patient at Children's Hospital of Pittsburgh and fifth in the nation, this led to a certain amount of news coverage involving her case. One of the nurses, Karen, was watching the news one night before she had to go back to work. The news was talking about Tara, and Karen had thought, *I hope I don't get that transplant patient*. Sure enough the next day Karen was assigned to Tara! She was Karen's first double-lung patient to care for, and she didn't want to mess up. Karen did a wonderful job with professionalism and calmness, which put Tara at ease.

After the transplant, the road to recovery was made with much effort on Tara's behalf. There were physical therapy sessions to help rebuild muscles which had not been used for sometime, the chore of getting bathed and dressed for the day with assistance, and the constant battle to restore nutrition and gain weight. Tara was down to seventy-three pounds, like a rack of bones covered with skin! It was something for Mom to witness each day. Trying to help her with bathing and hair washing was heartbreaking, to say the least. It is ingrained in my mind forever.

One of the transplant coordinators, Jan, came not too long after Tara had been taken out of ICU and placed on the transplant floor, and she got Tara up to walk several times around the unit for the very first time. With weakness and wobbly legs, Tara did walk. Jan had asked her if she wanted to run and Tara said, "I don't know if I can." Almost falling down in the attempt to run, Tara did try.

Dad and Mom stood back in the doorway of her hospital room watching, moved to tears, and remarked, "If only the donor family could see Tara before and now!" As hard as it was for Tara to make this effort, we were thrilled to see her moving, realizing how far she had come and with hope for the future, not doubting for a moment, how thankful and grateful we were for our many great blessings that had occurred so far.

This same transplant coordinator has since told us how touched she was as she and Tara took that frail walk past the nurses station, because several of the nurses were crying. Jan was moved the same as the nurses were and said, "This is good for the whole team!" This was certainly uplifting for all to see.

In the same way the walk was uplifting, the food situation was anything but desirable. A dietician visited Tara frequently, stressing the overwhelming need to eat and gain weight. Tara would cry over this, as she simply was not able to eat at that point. Prior to surgery her appetite was almost nil. Tara would have Carnation Instant Breakfast drinks to supplement nutrition. She used to love a cooked egg but was unable even to eat the yolk, which says a lot for anyone trying to exist. While she would cook the egg she said it was like she was eating it right then so by the time she sat down to eat, she was full. Such a trying ordeal!

We parents would come into Tara's hospital room and ask how we could help with her menu, post-transplant, and, putting it mildly, the roof would go off the room! Tara could let us have it, where with the dietician she would only get frustrated and cry over it to us. They wanted her to consume 3,200 calories per day, and it was unrealistic for a small and recovering weak body.

One day a long time after surgery, we brought Tara a much loved Burger King Whopper. It took her two hours to finish eating it but she was pleased with the first step in her eating progress. Tara still speaks of this accomplishment yet today.

After much struggle and turmoil, in due time, Tara's appetite did return slowly. It was a whole tuna fish sandwich and two bags of Ruffles potato chips that sparked Tara's full-blown appetite. She had eaten a whole sandwich, which was unbelievable, and one bag of chips. She then asked her dad, "Could I have another bag of chips?" A much surprised dad went to the vending machine and did indeed bring Tara another bag of chips!

On the brighter side, we have met the girl, Shelly, from Tacoma, Washington, who was the first pediatric double-lung transplant patient done at Children's. She and her mom came less than two weeks following Tara's transplant. We have seen them on several occasions, and there is a special bond between the girls, and also between the parents and siblings of each family. The encouragement they gave was immeasurable. Shelly had been post-op for almost two years upon this meeting with Tara. To see another living person who was back in the mainstream of life, attending school, working, and enjoying life in general was extremely encouraging. She was someone who had gone through the same difficult world of transplantation and survived what Tara was just now beginning.

Follow-up visits were spent at the Ronald McDonald House until kids turned eighteen years of age, and then it was on to the Family Houses. This is an adjustment, as previously there had been lots of young people around, but the new situation for housing is mostly adults. Crossing over from child to adult also creates changes, but good times come as a result of these shifts. The privilege of leaving childhood behind and grasping for adulthood would not have been possible without transplantation.

Chapter Fourteen

Christmas

After a four-week hospitalization we still needed to stay in the Pittsburgh area, so the Ronald McDonald House was our home. At first with Christmas fast approaching and talk of discharge from the hospital, Dr. Fricker said we could go home. I asked, "Do you mean *home* home?" His reply was, "Yes." I remember distinctly saying, "Oh no, we have to know what transplant life is like outside these hospital walls!" We felt we should not just check out of the hospital and head for Michigan where lung transplants were not common at the present time. We wondered how problems which could arrive at any given moment could possibly be treated back home. Our security was still in Children's Hospital, with all of this being so new to us, and we were somewhat apprehensive about being so far away from the knowledge of this fine facility.

Christmas shopping was done on foot as we were without a car, and we either walked or took the bus or cab to and from the hospital. When asked what Tara wanted for Christmas, she said, "I already have what I wanted, my new lungs!" That about said it for all of us. Tara receiving her lungs made our Christmas extra special as we anticipated every upcoming day to be special just because all four of our family members were still together.

The Christmas of 1990 is one we will always remember and one of the best we have ever experienced. Aunt Marilyn had given Tara a Christmas tree for her hospital room, and it now served a good purpose in our new room at the Ronald McDonald House. Cards and packages were coming from home. There were beautiful Christmas lights outside our home away from home, shining brightly from 500 Shady Avenue and creating a sight to behold for all to see. Inside the beautiful Victorian home, there was that extra special bonding with families who had come from far and near for the purpose of receiving help for their very ill loved ones. To add to the true Christmas spirit, there was a Christmas tree on three floors of the house which we had grown to love and call home. As we have said many times, we were not alone. Christmas and home can be anywhere we are sent, and this year we were sent to Pittsburgh just like all the other families under this very same roof.

Following discharge from the hospital, shortly after Christmas, there was an episode in which Tara spiked a high fever, had vomiting, and was unable to keep her rejection medication down along with all other meds. The rejection medication is a must to keep her from rejecting the transplanted organs, so with all these symptoms, back to the hospital we went for a duration of three weeks. Tara had developed CMV (cytomegalovirus) and needed extensive treatment for ninety days post-transplant, still in Pittsburgh. After being admitted to the hospital that second time, Dr. Fricker looked at me and said, "It's a good thing you didn't go home!" We would have had to be flown right back to Pittsburgh after just arriving home home. The reason they suggested going home home in the first place was to let Tara celebrate Christmas at home, and the suggestion was said in wanting only the best for Tara. That would have been fine if everything had gone well, but it didn't. I still don't know how we could have had this prior insight, but somehow we did realize things could go terribly wrong in just a very short while, and we wanted to be in the best possible place for proper treatment. It must have been God telling us to stay put, cool our heels, and once again sit back and see how things went regarding the recovery process.

Upon discharge this second time, a home care nurse came to the Ronald McDonald House for Tara's further treatment. Without this unexpected complication, we probably would have returned to Michigan sooner. All things happen for a reason, so I guess we were meant to be away from home a while longer. We remained in Pittsburgh for three and a half months.

Christmas was spent in Pittsburgh and people would ask us, "Don't you want to be home for Christmas?"

We would answer, "No, this is where we are meant to be." The Ronald McDonald House was filled with families just like us in similar circumstances, so we were not alone. We have met so many beautiful people, and our lives have been touched and enriched by sharing with others who also have life-threatening illnesses.

We could only hang onto our faith which had carried us to this stage, knowing God was taking each step of the journey with us.

When Tara's health allowed, a tutor came to the Ronald McDonald House for her school work to be completed. Sometimes she was able to do this, and often the tutor had to be postponed until she felt up to it. Tara was still pushing herself, as she had always done, and there were days when she just told herself she was up to doing school work, but not really. It was nice to have a tutor available for the students, and there were several kids at the house who took advantage of these great services provided by the Pittsburgh community. It seemed that with every need we had away from home, there was a way to have these needs met.

Derek continued on with his classes at the school right down the street from the Ronald McDonald House. He would visit Tara in the hospital when he could; other times another family at the house would sort of keep an eye on him until we returned from the hospital. He caught his hand in the treadmill once and, on a more serious note, fell out of a tree nearby, and we had to take him to the hospital. Derek was the patient this time. So being away from home did not make us in any way exempt from accidents happening, and you just had to go with the flow, no matter what took place.

Chapter Fifteen

Extended Family

Another day in the hospital we will always remember with mixed feelings was the viewing of Tara's very own lungs they had removed to make way for the new healthy set of lungs. Lynne Cipriani had previously arranged for this meeting with the pathologist and she, along with Tara, Dad, Mom, and brother Derek entered the pathology room for the special event which was about to take place. Tara's very diseased lungs had been placed on a tray before us. She proceeded to put rubber gloves on and then reached for her lungs to hold them. This was very touching for her family members to see, and what her thoughts were at that moment may never be known. We were also gloved and could hold these lungs too. I asked myself why was this such a strange feeling, all of us looking at and holding Tara's lungs; after all, they had been part of her existence for the past fourteen years! Not too many people could say their hands had held their own lungs! The picture of this event is also tucked away in Tara's photo album and I look at this quite often, just to take a trip down memory lane as a reminder of how far we have all come since facing the realization that we really did have a great big problem to deal with and what avenues we had to travel to seek help. These avenues have brought us to a level we never would have reached in our lives without this devastating challenge to cope with, both spiritually and with deep feelings which take us to the core of real living. It makes one do actual soul searching and choose a better way of life, helping others if there is a way possible for us to do so.

Our transplant coordinator and special friend, Lynne Cipriani, whom we have grown to love dearly, accompanied us that day of viewing the lungs, and it was so good she could share a special time in all our lives. Lynne is a very special lady, gives more than 100 percent in her job, goes above and beyond the call of duty, and extends herself in such a beautiful way, and you could not help but to fall in love with her.

Tara wrote a term paper while still in high school which was a wonderful tribute to Lynne. She spoke of the kindness, caring, and concern for the patients which is so evident as one watches Lynne go about her daily work. Tara has said she wanted to be as much like Lynne as she could when she entered the work force of her chosen field, something related to the medical profession. Tara and our family admire the dedication Lynne has with her profession. The personal touch she adds to families, her quick twinkle of the eyes, and her smile helps make her the person we so much adore and hold close in our hearts.

Lynne had been a nurse in the intensive care unit prior to accepting the job of transplant coordinator. This new job had just started for her when here came Tara for what was considered to be a heart-lung transplant. Tara was her very first transplant patient, and there is a bond between Tara and Lynne that will always be there. There could be praise for her throughout this book, but I am afraid we would run out of words to describe just how special Lynne is to our family. She is truly a trouper in her field, and what would Children's Hospital of Pittsburgh do without her! Other families must have experienced the same thoughts as we have had regarding the closeness and love of this very special person.

The social worker at Children's Hospital, Laura Hangard, is also a very special friend who has helped us tremendously. It is through her efforts and caring that we were able to be guests at the Ronald McDonald House for our entire stay in the area and the majority of subsequent follow-up visits since. She has assisted us several times since coming home in getting airline tickets, at no cost, for our frequent visits back for follow-up. We drive when we can, but sometimes due to weather conditions, etcetera, we are unable to make the trip without the plane arrangements she schedules for us. This is such a relief to families, and is that much less financially to worry about. We are truly grateful to Laura for her love and friendship. If there is a problem of any sort, all one has to do is turn to Laura and she will find a way to make it easier for all concerned. When we arrived in Pittsburgh for Tara's transplant, our son, Derek, needed a place to attend school while in the area. It was Laura Hangard who thought of the school just down the street from the Ronald McDonald House, as it was close and he could walk to and from school. Because Derek was homesick and sometimes wanted to go *home* home, it could be thought that Derek was not pleased with school. It was not the case; at that time he could see no other school than the one back home! We have since told Laura, "Derek wouldn't have liked any school other than his own."

As was mentioned previously, when Derek fell out of the tree and was incoherent at times, he said, "Tell Laura I'm sorry I didn't like my school!" You see, he had to make it right by Laura and somehow in his own way explain his feelings, which he did not express very often. He kept things pretty much wrapped up inside. Once again, if it hadn't been for Laura's arrangement for school, Derek would not have had his needs met regarding his continuing education while away from home.

Laura has helped us in so many countless ways, too numerous to even remember, but we do know we treasure her and will always love her; we hold her close in thought and in our hearts.

Dr. Jay Fricker, one of the best in his field of cardiology, relocated to Florida, and do we ever miss him! Other staff physicians who have lovingly cared for Tara are Dr. Susan Miller, Dr. Boyle, Dr. Park, and later on, Dr. Law.

We must always remember Dr. Marian Michaels as the infections occur—and rest assured they are present at times. This very special friend, with her fantastic expertise, knows how to treat her patients to get them over the critical stages and on to recovery. Her team physicians are also well qualified, and we feel secure with the knowledge this fine department has available for us and other families.

The nurses who so lovingly cared for Tara are a great group of people. At this time, there was Debbie, Beth, Renee, Pat, Claudia, Christy, two Amys, four Karens, Terry, Jill, Kim, and more. Some of them are still there, and we still see them; others have changed positions, married, or moved away. These people are regarded as friends who will always be remembered as being there when the going was rough and who helped to make things better. They do not just do their so-called job, they give of themselves in making patients feel comfortable in strange surroundings. Their goal is the patients' well-being first, and this is shown with personal touches, something so very important in the recovery of the patient and his or her family. From the housekeeping department, David added his own personal caring as he cleaned the room daily, smiled, and asked if everything was okay. The dietary department did an excellent job too, along with smiles and words of encouragement. The entire staff at Children's should be commended for a job well done along with making the families feel at home, at least as close to home as you can be under very trying circumstances.

We cannot find enough good to say about this special hospital up on the hill in Pittsburgh, Pennsylvania. The staff have become extended family to us, and we look forward with anticipation to our follow-up visits, as long as everything checks out okay and we can return *home* home. They too show their pleasure in seeing the patients and family members again.

They are certainly a terrific group of very special people to whom we give our thanks for making us feel special and loved.

Some of the nurses from 9 North including
Terry, Debbie, Karen, Jill and Beth with Tara.

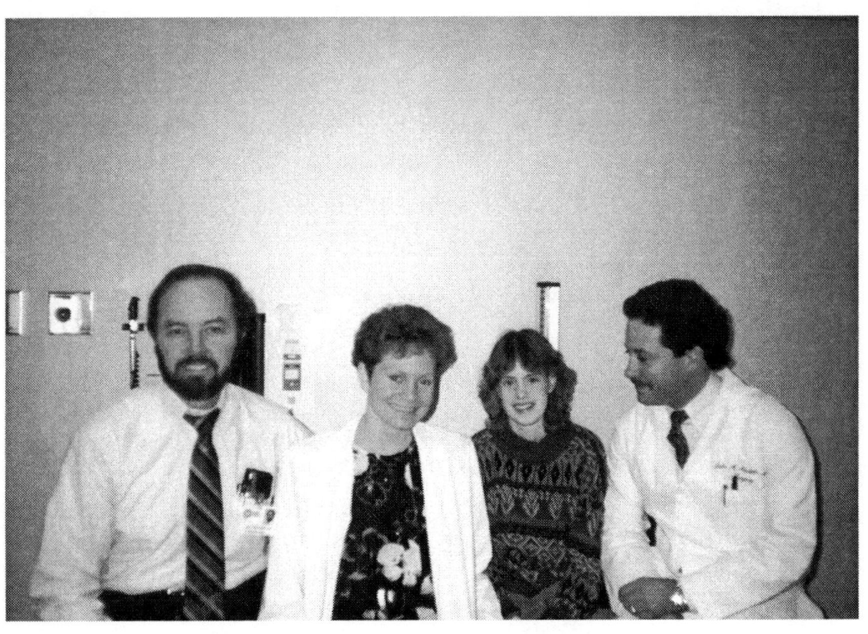

Dr. Jay Fricker - cardiologist, PITT;
Lynne Cipriani - transplant co-ordinator, PITT;
Tara, and Dr. John Armitage - cardiovascular surgeon, PITT

Tara with Dr. Boyle, cardiologist, PITT

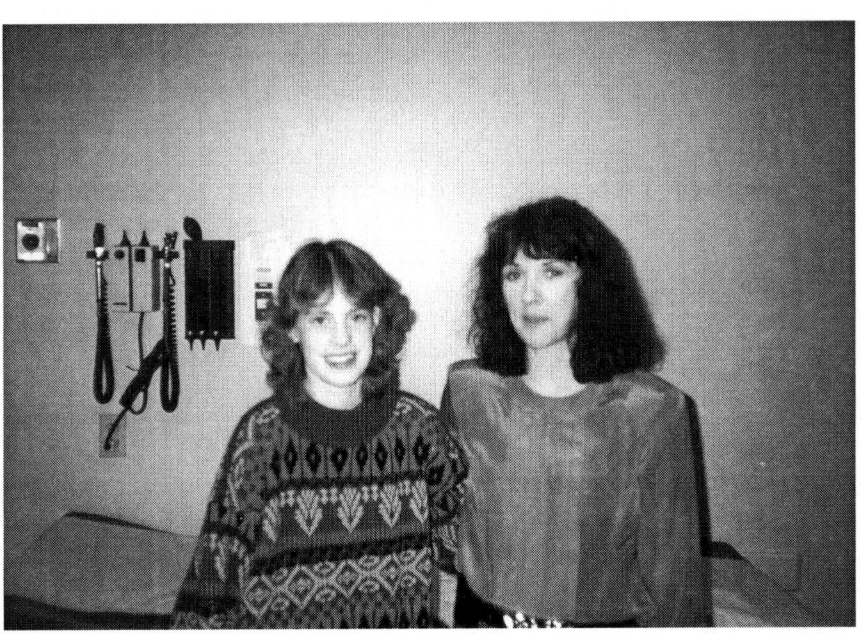

Tara with Laura Hangard - social worker

Chapter Sixteen

Dr. Kurland, a Special Pulmonologist

We have been privileged to meet a very special pulmonologist at Children's Hospital, as he gives his medical knowledge mixed with his very own wit and charm. One wonders where he came from and what brought him to this destination. One thing is for sure, we are glad he did come!

Tara says, "Dr. Kurland is awesome, he is the best, he knows when to be serious and when to joke around." He is highly intelligent, enjoys culture, and is very knowledgeable in both medicine and the humanities.

Upon seeing Dr. Kurland in the hospital halls or entering the patient's room, the most distinguished ties he wears bring out the different sides to his unique personality! Even though he is not always the pulmonologist to see Tara on follow-up visits, he manages somehow to see her before she leaves the hospital and this makes the visits complete. Our whole family thoroughly enjoys seeing him; he is a bright spot in our lives, and we have the utmost respect for him. We are thankful he has become Tara's doctor and a friend to each member of our family.

After flashing his broad smile, his wave of the hand, and "How have you been, have you heard any new jokes?" he then tells a joke of his own, gives a hug, and ends by saying, "Keep rock'n!" Funny thing Tara's speciality is rocking in her recliner chair, looking out the window of our living room, watching the cars zoom down the freeway, collecting her thoughts, and waiting patiently for the day when she can be up and about, free as a bird again and feeling in good health.

Someday soon maybe Tara will say, "I want to run!" or maybe there will be new remarks said the second time around. The circle

Dr. Kurland, pulmonologist, PITT

of life continues, and how many twists and turns there will be in the road ahead remains to be seen.

Yes, Dr. Kurland is one of a kind, teaching his art of performing the bronchoscopies with such excellency. Needless to say, Tara gave him quite a problem with cooperating because she would cough and talk repetitively, making Dr. Kurland's job very stressful. After Tara would wake up in the Same Day Surgery Unit, Dr. Kurland would come in, run his hands through his black hair, and tussle it up in many different directions in an attempt to let us know, "Boy, that was a toughie."

Tara remembers that when she woke up during one of the bronchoscopies she turned her head towards the screen and could see right into her airway. She tried to tell Dr. Kurland how awesome it was, but could not speak because the scope was running between her vocal cords. Dr. Kurland said, "No fair talking!" Tara doesn't remember anything else until waking in the Same Day Unit. Dr. Kurland always handled situations with ease no matter what the problem seemed to be.

Along with the "Keep rock'n," Dr. Kurland would use the "live long and prosper" sign from Star Trek to let Tara know this is what he wants for her. His enthusiasm for life is truly catching. He loves life and lives it to the fullest. He knows that life can end at any given moment and life is a precious gift. Dr. Kurland is loved and admired tremendously by Tara and the rest of us. No words could ever explain how much he means to us. If we tried it would fail miserably. Again, a big thank you, Dr. Kurland, and lots of love to you! Don't forget to "Keep rock'n!"

Chapter Seventeen

Leaving Pittsburgh

On March 7, 1991, we packed our belongings, shared in a delicious ham dinner which was lovingly prepared for us at the Ronald McDonald House, said our farewells to the new friends we had made both at the house and at the hospital, and boarded the plane for home home.

The sky this particular day was sunny and clear. Tara's bright smile was also filled with sunshine in her heart and radiated for all to see. God had carried us thus far, and we will continue to praise Him for His blessings.

We had waited for this day to arrive and were filled with excitement and anticipation. Now that this magic day had become a reality, we had mixed feelings and emotions about leaving our home away from home. Leaving the safety net of the hospital surroundings and wondering if we could survive in the outside world was more than a little scary. Like a butterfly breaking out of its cocoon and wanting to fly, as Tara said by mouthing the words while still on the respirator, "I want to run!" We must now run, remembering the poem Footprints.

The friendships made will be present in our hearts forever, and we still hear from several families on special occasions, mostly at Christmas.

One family, mom Deb, dad Skip, and daughter Christy from Ohio, even attended Tara's graduation open house at our home in Michigan. We were surprised and deeply touched by them caring so much to put forth effort to share in our happiness at such a special time in all our lives.

We were planning on doing the same thing when their daughter, Christy, graduated from high school, making the trip to Ohio for open house celebration at their home. I was still recuperating from the accident which occurred that winter, plus it was Derek's high school graduation too. We were disappointed we could not attend this happy occasion, but sent a gift along with our best wishes.

Graduations for transplant patients are big milestones, and these kids have achieved this honor against all odds. They have reached this point in their lives, having to struggle to keep up with studies along with poor health. Most of the other students have not had their lives put on hold, waiting for organs to come and restored health. Again, we have so much to be thankful for and have learned not to take everything for granted, as we once did.

Special guests at Tara's open house also included a transplant patient, back in school and herself waiting to graduate in a couple of years. Christy now is looking healthy, and we did not recognize them at first when they drove in the driveway. It wasn't until we saw Christy's mom, Deb, smile that we realized just who they were and could not believe what we were seeing!

This is just one of many families who had been brought together by a common bond in a special place called Pittsburgh, Pennsylvania.

We see these families as we are all going back to the hospital for routine check-ups. Often times these friends are the only people who really know what you are going through, for they too have walked the same road.

Pittsburgh is such a special place to us, and with the frequent visits back to the hospital for follow-up, we almost left Michigan to take up permanent residency in the city. Upon considering everything, we finally decided whatever was "normal" still remained back home. Here we are, all four of us still together and very thankful for Tara's miracle which was sent from above.

You leave one world behind in Pittsburgh and enter another world back home and keep switching emotions, sometimes not knowing where you really belong!

Chapter Eighteen

Back Home

We made the decision not to let people know our plane was arriving home, as the yard may have been full of friends when we reached our destination. That would have been very meaningful and a sight to remember, but we chose to come home to the house we left three and a half months previously and collect our thoughts quietly.

A peaceful night of sleep was spent in our own home, content and happy along with counting our many blessings. The following morning I asked, "Does this feel like home?" We all agreed it was definitely home for all to enjoy and for which to be grateful.

The welcome in the following days and weeks was unbelievable. There were so many expressions of love, caring, and concern along with happiness for all of us. Our lives were made richer by everyone we touched and by those who touched us along the path we took in getting Tara healthy again. Her quality of life is great, and she can go out into the world and spread the word of how good God has been with His great blessing!

Entering school again for both Tara and Derek was scary and exciting at the same time. Being away so long and now seeing old friends and getting back in the swing of things at home was truly refreshing!

My husband, Ron, just had temporary work at the time, and he remained with us for the entire time we were in Pittsburgh. Such a rock he has been, very supportive and always present. I would not have wanted to go through this without him at our side. We were all thankful for the love of dad and husband, as he was very much needed when trying to cope through the rough times and sharing in the good times. Sometimes a parent has tried to go back home and work, but finds he or she left feelings back at the hospital where the child is receiving treatment. It is not easy having the rest of the family together and one attempting work back home. How wonderful we were all together!

I returned to work in our local hospital where the employees had given their vacation days so there would be a paycheck for us. I told them they needed their own vacation days, as they worked hard and vacation time should be for themselves and their families. They replied, "We can't take it away, Betty, but let us do what we can to help." I will always treasure this act of love and friendship and know they gave so much in our time of need. You do not always find this out in the workplace, and we thank them tremendously for caring. May God richly bless each one as they have blessed our family.

Chapter Nineteen

Bree-An, New Family Member

Tara had expressed the wish to have a puppy in her life, a pup she could hold for the rest of its whole life. Looking ahead to the future our search leaned toward finding a miniature schnauzer, which we had decided could fit into our family mold.

The first Christmas following our return home from Pittsburgh, after viewing her gifts and seeing no puppy, Tara was more than a little disappointed; in fact she was indignant about not receiving the only gift she had asked for that particular year. We had told her we were following the newspapers and there was an advertisement for schnauzers, but we had not yet made the call.

With the holiday season past, we hoped things would settle down a bit and could devote time for training a pet along with enforcing discipline, which is very time consuming. A great deal of energy and effort must be given in such an undertaking, but we felt ready! Ready or not, we said we would now take the plunge and move on with some hesitation, although we were eager to find a new member of our family. The efforts put forth are well worth it, but trying indeed, and one does get slightly frazzled in the process.

The right time had come, or so we thought. Mom placed the telephone call and asked, "Do you still have a female schnauzer left?"

The reply was, "Yes we do." That is all we needed to hear and Dad, Mom, Tara, and Derek headed to the car for our next adventure!

Bree-An had already been picked out by Tara for a name to be given her puppy, and Bree-An she did find this very same day. All five of us arrived home to begin our bonding and getting acquainted with each other. With this training behind us eventually, such joys followed and Bree-An blessed us beyond measure!

Tara said, "Bree-An is a true companion. She listens and doesn't say a word back but the expressions on her face say a load and a half. When I'm down she comes over, puts her paws on the arm of my rocking chair, and gives me those looks that are enough to let me know she cares. Then in reply I pet her little silver feet with so much love in return. Bree-An is truly a gift from God and I feel very lucky to have such a wonderful dog to comfort me through the days. I love my little pumpkin a ton!"

We love her dearly even with her excessive barking when company arrives, upon seeing a bird fluttering in the yard, or at any other distraction she feels is not wanted around our house. She feels this is her domain, I guess, as she is fiercely protective of her loved ones as is her nature. Bree-An is so loyal to us and always shows her unconditional love with her "Woo, woo, woo" as we enter our home after busy days at school and work.

Have we been rewarded and blessed beyond what words can describe, certainly! Bree-An came into our home and stole our hearts without even trying!

Chapter Twenty

Make-a-Wish

A year and a half after Tara's transplant, she was back in school and in the mainstream of life again. Our family was adjusting to being back home, we were busy with the school activities, attending church each Sunday, and in general just trying to play catch-up from being almost in a different world for the past several months. The trips back to Pittsburgh help to keep us in focus of our new existence and yet are a reminder of being forever, for the duration of life, whatever that may be! For anyone who cannot seem to be flexible, pack up and make the trips, come home again and know you are going again soon, this could be a big problem. Families who have experienced this take it in their stride, do the necessary follow-up, and be thankful there is a reason for the trip. Tara is still here to need the continuing care and how life would not be the same without her here with us.

This past winter I was filling in for a maternity leave position, once again getting back to the medical transcriptionist job I always enjoyed. I hadn't been involved in this capacity for a few years and wondered how I would meet this new challenge. Well, I did find the medical words were still with me. I was maybe a little rusty with the speed end of it but I realized, as I had always known, this was my first love for a career! I started out at age eighteen, straight from high school, and was thrust right into a position at our local hospital. Learning the difficult language was indeed trying, but with determination on my part, the wonderful boss I had to give me encouragement by her example taught me plenty. I saw Eleanor work and work, giving so much of herself to her job and said to myself, *If Eleanor can do this, I would certainly like to be a transcriptionist too.* Back then one did not have to have a degree, you learned as you went while performing your duties each day. I saw Eleanor's dedication and devotion each and every day, and she gave me more confidence in myself, which I definitely was lacking! I feel everything I know in this field I owe to Eleanor! Once again I was enjoying the good feeling of doing the work I always loved, if only for a short while.

While attempting to carry out the commitment of this new temporary job, my dad fell and ended up in the hospital in a near-by larger city, never regaining consciousness, had to be taken off the respirator, and passed away two weeks later. I was trying to work, visit Dad, and keep up at home with our family. It was a stressful time again for us. It seemed the stress would just not go away, it followed us wherever we went! God was trying to teach us with the challenges, letting us know He was near constantly. All we had to do was trust in Him. He never said there wouldn't be trials, it is how we handle the situations dealt to us.

Grandpa Lewis did get to see Tara receive her transplant, and was he thrilled to see her health again! While we were in Pittsburgh, my dad and his friend Virginia checked on our house to see that everything was okay. We were not worried about our house and as Ron said, "If anything is going to happen, we would not want to be there anyway!" This is another example of setting priorities and of what is important in life, that being just Life. I am happy Grandpa was able to witness Tara's renewed good health before he left this world. Both Grandpa and Grandma Peters also have enjoyed still seeing Tara blossom with enthusiasm for continued life.

After all of this—Dad passing, my tour of duty ending with the temporary job, Ron still not having steady work, and Tara and Derek through school for the year—we decided we were ready for the Make-a-Wish trip which had been suggested to us several months earlier.

Any child under the age of eighteen with a life-threatening illness may have a wish of their choice through the Make-a-Wish Foundation, the funding being given by private individuals and organizations to help make these children happy and somehow ease all the unknowns for a short while. What a wonderful cause to donate to Make-a-Wish, knowing one is helping to make a child's wish come true. Many of these children go on living, but some of them receive their wish and then quietly slip away, having done what was so very special to them.

It was Tara's wish to visit Hawaii, see Pearl Harbor and Diamond Head, and take in the beauty of a faraway land. Through the generosity of this fine organization, Make-a-Wish, we were given a vacation of a lifetime! This would certainly have been out of reach for our family without contributions to such a worthwhile cause.

The dream of going to Hawaii became a reality on June 8, 1991. Tara, along with her dad, mom, and brother Derek, left for an eight-day vacation. The island of Maui became our refuge for a week. We were away from it all, grateful and thankful to still be all together.

Such beauty we had never experienced and at times it seemed unreal. We wondered if we were really there or still dreaming?

Tara did indeed celebrate her sixteenth birthday in beautiful Hawaii, truly a gorgeous place in the sun for such a special occasion. Not everyone gets to spend their birthday in such great fashion, and the circumstances as to why we were even there made it much more meaningful. The days were filled with plans which had been made by this organization: a luau (Hawaiian feast), snorkeling, dinner at the Hard Rock Cafe, a spectacular helicopter ride over the island, and a visit to Pearl Harbor and Diamond Head.

After the long plane ride of many hours, we arrived at Honolulu and were met by a beautiful tour guide who was both gracious and kind. We then purchased a rental car to go see Pearl Harbor and Diamond Head. Both were quite an experience to say the least. To see the sunken ships of the past and to imagine the horrendous horror that must have been present as they went down can not be expressed in words. It had a tremendous effect on all of us.

For the big birthday bash, we gave Tara a birthday cake along with red roses. She had an attempted swim in the ocean, but the huge waves pulled her end over end repeatedly, and this was extremely frustrating. Ron and Derek frolicked in the beautiful warm waters of the Pacific. They thoroughly enjoyed Hawaii and both vow to return again, really wanting this to be home some day! We all changed for the evening, each of us in our new matching Maui T-shirts, and arrived for the luau where Tara was seated in the front row of one of the tables along with the rest of her family. There was live entertainment for all to remember because it was with exotic Polynesian dancers. The pig roast was unique, unusual to us, and had a taste all of its own. I think one would have to acquire a taste for this so-called delicacy. Some of us did enjoy the pork and other deliciously prepared dishes. One cannot go to Hawaii and not mention the succulent pineapple which is plentiful and simply marvelous. Nothing we have at home even resembles this sweetness! We could have had a steady diet of only pineapple, we loved the taste. What a wonderful evening! We went back to our hotel room tired, happy, and thankful, and snuggled in for the night for some much needed sleep. In the meantime, Tara had purchased leis for her special doctors and nurses at the hospital, to be taken to Pittsburgh on our upcoming visit. We took pictures of each one with Tara, a lei around the neck, for the ongoing photo album which we treasure, as this tells the whole story.

When the time came to leave this heaven here on earth, not really wanting to go, we promised each other we would try somehow at some point to return, if only in our dreams. Through this journey, we have been places and met people beyond our horizons.

Tara says, "Hawaii is a very pretty place and a trip I never thought I would be able to take. I am so thankful to Make-a-Wish for making my dream come true." So many caring people reach out and give hope and happiness, and we are just one family who has received such pleasure, putting aside the trying times of coping for the moment. We will always cherish this most special time together in a paradise called Hawaii, with a beauty all its own. All this was made possible completely by Make-a-Wish Foundation.

It is our wish to be able some day to help provide a wish for another family in similar circumstances. It is simply our way of giving back that special love and caring we received in so many ways. We are forever grateful to Make-a-Wish Foundation!

Chapter Twenty-one

Setting Priorities

Upon our arrival back to Pittsburgh, we get settled in wherever we are staying, usually have a day free to rest, go out to eat, and sometimes take in a movie. It is nice to not feel rushed with appointments the very next day. We have this day to do as we please, and it seems to make it easier for us Monday morning when we begin with the follow-up at the hospital. There are the routine check-up visits with the transplant coordinator, Lynne Cipriani, along with whatever doctors are on call for each service Tara is involved in. The next day is the scheduled bronchoscopy, the checking of the transplanted lungs to see if there is rejection. We then see our special friends, hear the "Hi Tara!" several times a day at the elevators, and visit the transplant floor to see the nurses who mean so much to Tara.

Once the solid two-day hospital routine has been covered, while waiting for the test results for possible rejection, we can do some so-called normal activities. We still do fun things as a family and every day is not a downer. Someone told us about an amusement park in Pittsburgh called Kennywood. We were unaware such a place existed for a year or so after Tara's surgery, but once we found this unique park, it was one of the top priorities for us to include in our summer trip. What a thrilling time! There are rides of every sort for all kinds of people, from young to the older, food galore to satisfy your appetite, and a cool refreshing drink to quench your thirst while enjoying your favorite resting spot. Back to the rides until the next stop. It is a fun but sometimes tiring outing. Everyone in our family thoroughly enjoys the Thunderbolt roller coaster! The Raging Rapids is a cool and soaking ride, but make sure you wear clothes lighter in weight, so you dry faster. Otherwise, you have soggy clothes for the duration of the time there, that is, until you finally do dry out. It is not the best feeling in the world to be soaked clean through, but it is well worth it! In the meantime, there is always cotton candy, which is one of Tara's favorites! For those of us who are brave enough to attempt it, it is on to the Steel Phantom! This roller coaster is higher than any other there, and is one of the highlights of the park but definitely scary to some. One has to work his or her courage up to that level of excitement in order to even consider such a challenge. Ron and Derek first came up with enough nerve and stamina to tackle the monster of a ride. They came back to us with smiles from ear to ear, hair flung in disarray, and talking a mile a minute explaining what they had just experienced.

A couple of years later, Derek asked Tara to take the ride with him. It was after dark, which made it even more unknown as to how it would turn out, but Tara did decide to go for it! With shaky legs and heart pounding, Tara boarded the seat with her brother by her side. Derek was encouraging her that everything would be okay, and Derek was a source of comfort. There were lights on the track except for the biggest dip that looked like you were going to crash into the ground, but you knew the track continued. Then came the loops! What a heart-jolting ride. As for me, I didn't even want to think about it! No ifs, ands, or buts, it was settled on my part. I do not even like roller coasters, but wanting to be with the family and sharing in the pleasure, I can part-way enjoy the smaller ones, or at least tolerate them. There is a feeling of flying through the air and nothing really describes it, just that you are always waiting for the next jolt, twist, and turn, and hoping the track and seats remain intact and everyone will be safe.

Once the final test results are given, we receive the all clear signal, and are told we can then leave for home, we usually go home the following morning. We have an all-day trip back home, a couple of meals on the way, drinks included, which makes us hit several rest areas along the way, so depending on how many stops we make determines the length of time we take to get to our home. It is always good to arrive home, but we also enjoy the trips as much as we can.

The things we used to worry about are no longer as important. When I previously heard the words "Take one day at a time!"

it was very upsetting to me, as we were aware of our own feelings. Words are easy for someone else to say to you; in those well meant words, sometimes it is only talk if one has not lived through this roller coaster world, the ups and downs of always facing the unknown. It is actually about never feeling settled, wondering what will take place next, and trusting everything is as okay as it can be under these conditions. Finally, when I was ready to accept everything and not everyone else stating their thoughts on the matter, in my own mind it then became, "One moment or one second at a time!"

Life is so precious, and we do take many things for granted. Once our health is taken away, only then do we realize what we had before and now miss. In the process of healing, what we do with this idle time in our lives depends on us. Recently, as I was recuperating for eight months, during my time spent confined to the house I tried to figure out what God wanted me to do in the future. I asked Him to reveal this to me and I would do my best to carry out His wishes and also make them mine.

Tara is now waiting for God to let her know what He wants her to do for the future. Many times in the hospital she has been asked to go and speak to families who were either waiting for a transplant or were newly transplanted and still wondering what the quality of life would be post-transplant.

Through our experience in the transplant world, we have been encouraged beyond measure upon seeing someone post-operative arrive in our room, looking and appearing ever so healthy. What hope we were given and our spirits soared! Tara has given many families that same hope we were given and that hope is better than anything even hospital staff can share with you. Actually seeing a person who has gone back to school or re-entered the workforce, who is functioning very well and living a productive life is all the hope one needs. This also gives the patient a common goal to strive for and incentive to never give up, just keep pushing for return of health.

Yes, your priorities do change and you find a "new normal" as compared to the old normal we once had in our existence.

Now six and one-half years later, we have indeed seen Tara grow up into adulthood. What a privilege to see her blossom into a beautiful young lady, filled with courage, who entered college in pursuit of those dreams!

It has already been eight months since Tara has been unable to attend college. She is once again sitting at home waiting for the all important hospital call to come saying, "Tara's lungs are here!"

The journey continues on with hope and thankfulness for who we still have in our lives, including our daughter and sister. God has allowed her to stay here on Earth, He must not be ready for her in His heavenly home, not just yet.

1997 graduation at Alma College
Tara with Jon, Kelly, Sarah, and Curtis

Tara, Rebekah, Kari, Hannah, Erin, and Karla
July, 1996 at the Student Institute for Campus Ministry
in Bellingham, WA

Rebecca and Lonna with Tara
Spring 1997 - Alma College friends—park in Alma, MI

Chapter Twenty-two

The Unknown Again

Tara graduated with honors along with the rest of her high school class in 1994. We were thrilled for this day and proud of how far she had come and whom she had become. Yes she had accomplished this goal in achieving part of her dreams.

Then it was off to Alma College, anticipating the thoughts of a career in medicine. Even though this college was near our home, Tara stayed in the dorm and experienced community living, so to speak. We needed to let Tara go, and she needed to let go of us. We have given it our best shot not to smother Tara, as it would be easy to do, given the circumstances we have shared. Tara had the transplant to live, and within reason we have let her do just that! Two years were completed. She went only two weeks of her junior year and developed pneumonia plus a bacterial infection and had to put college on hold for now.

Not one to give in easily, Tara kept trying to attend classes, work part-time in the college library, and did her best to do so-called activities of daily living. Her instructors and friends had to keep saying, "Tara, go home and get rested and well." This drive she has is good most of the time, but sometimes not so good. Tara has never half done anything, it is all or nothing! We have said this about her as a small child, and she still exhibits these fine qualities which carry her through the obstacles she has met along the journey.

Tara has been placed back on the nationwide transplant list for a second double lung transplant. After having been given six healthy, wonderful years, it is difficult to understand why it is being taken away a second time, but everything happens for a reason.

Once again Tara is patiently waiting for God to show her what He wants to do with her life and what plans He has for her future.

There are feelings Tara has deep down in the corners of her heart that even her parents and brother will never know. Likewise we have feelings which no one other than us can possibly express. Those who have been there and lost children, or those in the situation where the possibility is so real, as in our case, certainly could comprehend the reality of it all or at least try to understand.

We have the pager, awaiting the call for Tara's lungs. We want them to come and yet fear the unknown to some extent. We must sit back and wait and continue to pray for Thy will to be done. We ask for comfort and peace along with God's loving arms wrapped securely around each of us as only He can do. Throughout different states, prayers are being said and we know they are being heard.

Tara's college friends, Sarah, Kelly, Jon, Erin, Rebecca, Lonna, Robin, Curtis, Ben, and several more have been a true blessing, as they listen, lend their support, and offer their love and prayers. It was through Chi Alpha, their Christian group on campus, that Tara learned about and received her salvation. Tara has learned to put everything aside and look towards Jesus to be her Lord to take care of everything that she is not big enough to fix. Back in chapter eighteen I said, "...she can go out into the world and spread the word of how good God has been with His great blessing!" Tara would say, "I can go out into the world and spread the word of how good God has been with His many, many great blessings!" Tara's faith is unshakable! Words cannot even begin to express what God means to her. Tara said, "He is so big and amazing that my infinitely small mind can't even begin to understand how to tell you what God means to me, so to try and explain to you would be a certain defeat! I know there is a reason for everything, and when I go to Pittsburgh I will get the chance to talk about God to more people, and if I die, then I will be with my Lord and Savior in Heaven. I can't lose either way. That is the cool part about being in tune with God."

Once, before a hospitalization in Pittsburgh, our living room was full of college friends wishing her well. We were leaving the following day, and Tara would be admitted upon arrival. Caring expressed often is the best medicine one can receive and cannot be replaced, other than with the actual medicine needed for survival. Tara has been on anti-rejection medications since her first transplant to keep her living and they are a must in her everyday plans.

Only God knows the future. We ask Him daily for His strength and His everlasting love.